Midjourney

From Concept to Creation: A Beginner's Guide to Midjourney Image Generation

by Sandro Schätz

Table of Contents

About the Author

I am a graphic designer with over a decade of experience, and my journey in this creative field has been both challenging and immensely rewarding. A few years back, I embraced artificial intelligence image generation as an essential tool to effectively keep pace with the rapidly evolving landscape of technology and to harness its potential for innovation and creativity. By integrating these innovative tools into my daily workflow, I not only enhance my creative process but also ensure that I remain relevant and competitive in this dynamic industry. This unique fusion of traditional design skills and cutting-edge AI technology allows me to push the boundaries of my work, creating truly unique visual solutions that resonate deeply with clients and diverse audiences alike. I am confident that my comprehensive understanding of this topic will greatly assist you in grasping the potential and excitement of this transformative technology!

Chapter 1: Introduction to Midjourney

What is Midjourney? - Provide a simple definition of Midjourney and its purpose as an AI image-generation tool.

Midjourney is an advanced artificial intelligence image-generation tool designed to transform textual prompts into visually striking images. It operates at the intersection of creativity and technology, allowing users to produce unique artwork based solely on their written descriptions. By leveraging deep learning algorithms and vast datasets, Midjourney interprets language to generate images that can range from the surreal to the hyper-realistic, catering to various artistic styles and preferences. This capability makes it an invaluable resource for individuals seeking to enhance their visual content without requiring extensive artistic skills.

The primary purpose of Midjourney is to democratize the art of image creation. Traditionally, producing high-quality visuals required a significant investment in time, skill, and resources. With Midjourney, anyone with a creative idea can generate bespoke images quickly and efficiently. This tool supports a wide array of users, including bloggers looking to enhance their written content with original visuals, content creators seeking unique graphics for their social media platforms, and artists exploring new avenues of creative expression. By streamlining the image generation process, Midjourney opens up new possibilities for visual storytelling.

Midjourney functions by employing a user-friendly interface that allows individuals to input their ideas in the form of prompts. These prompts can be descriptive, imaginative, or even abstract, and the AI interprets them to create images that reflect the user's vision. The tool's ability to understand context and nuance in language enables it to produce images that not only align with user expectations but also surprise and inspire. This makes it particularly appealing for graphic designers and artists who want to push the boundaries of their creative projects.

Midjourney offers a variety of customization options, allowing users to refine their outputs based on specific styles, colors, and themes. This flexibility is essential for professionals who require images that fit within particular branding guidelines or artistic frameworks. The tool's adaptability means that it can cater to diverse niches, whether it be generating illustrations for a children's book, creating promotional graphics for a product launch, or designing captivating visuals for an online portfolio. As a result, Midjourney serves as a powerful ally in the creative process.

In summary, Midjourney is more than just an AI image generator; it is a transformative tool that empowers users to bring their ideas to life through visual art. Its purpose lies in making image generation accessible to a broader audience, enabling creativity without the constraints of traditional artistic skills. As individuals continue to explore the capabilities of Midjourney, they will discover not only its practical applications but also its potential to inspire a new wave of artistic expression across various mediums and platforms.

The Role of Image Generation in the Digital Era - Explain how AI-generated images are used in modern content creation, including art, marketing, and social media.

The digital era has ushered in a transformative wave of technological advancements, particularly in the realm of image generation. AI-generated images are at the forefront of this revolution, fundamentally reshaping how content is created and consumed across various platforms. Artists, marketers, and social media influencers are increasingly turning to tools like Midjourney to enhance their visual storytelling.

In the world of art, AI-generated images offer a novel approach to creativity, enabling artists to push the boundaries of their imagination. By leveraging Midjourney's capabilities, artists can experiment with styles, colors, and compositions that they may not have considered otherwise. This technology not only serves as a source of inspiration but also acts as a collaborative partner in the creative process. Artists can generate multiple iterations of their ideas, selecting and refining the outputs to align with their vision. This synergy between human creativity and AI technology fosters an environment where traditional artistic practices meet innovative methods, leading to the emergence of unique artworks that may not be possible through conventional means.

In marketing, the impact of AI-generated images is profound. Brands are increasingly utilizing these images to create eye-catching advertisements and social media content that resonate with their target audiences. By generating high-quality visuals quickly, businesses can maintain a consistent presence across various platforms, enhancing brand recognition and engagement. Midjourney allows marketers to tailor images to specific campaigns or demographics, ensuring that visuals align with the message they wish to convey. This flexibility not only saves time and resources but also empowers brands to experiment with different aesthetics, optimizing their approach to capture consumer attention effectively.

Social media has become a visual-first medium, and the demand for compelling imagery is at an all-time high. AI-generated images play a crucial role in helping content creators stand out in a saturated landscape. By harnessing Midjourney's capabilities, influencers and bloggers can produce stunning visuals that complement their narratives and enhance audience engagement. These images can be customized to reflect personal styles or trends, making it easier for creators to maintain an authentic online presence. Additionally, the ability to generate images on demand allows for real-time content creation, enabling creators to respond swiftly to trends and audience preferences, thus keeping their content fresh and relevant.

The integration of AI-generated images into content creation democratizes artistry and design. Individuals without formal training or extensive resources can access powerful image generation tools, leveling the playing field in creative industries. Midjourney, with its user-friendly interface, equips aspiring artists and designers with the means to bring their ideas to life, regardless of their technical expertise. This accessibility fosters a new wave of creativity, encouraging diverse voices and perspectives to emerge in the digital landscape. As a result, the art and marketing sectors are enriched by a broader spectrum of creativity, further emphasizing the importance of AI-generated images in contemporary content creation.

The role of image generation in the digital era is multifaceted and far-reaching. From enhancing artistic expression to revolutionizing marketing strategies and enriching social media content, AI-generated images are integral to modern content creation. For those interested in harnessing the power of Midjourney, understanding these applications is crucial for maximizing the potential of their creative endeavors. As technology continues to evolve, the opportunities for innovation in image generation will only expand, making it an exciting time for artists, marketers, and content creators alike.

Why Use Midjourney? - Highlight the advantages of using Midjourney for creative projects.

Midjourney stands out as a powerful tool for creative projects, offering users an array of advantages that can significantly enhance their artistic endeavors. At its core, Midjourney utilizes advanced artificial intelligence to generate high-quality images based on textual prompts. This capability allows users to translate abstract concepts and ideas into visually compelling representations with remarkable ease. Whether you are a blogger looking to create eye-catching visuals for your content, an artist exploring new styles, or a graphic designer in need of unique imagery, Midjourney offers an accessible platform to bring your visions to life.

One of the primary benefits of using Midjourney is its user-friendly interface, which lowers the barrier to entry for individuals who may not possess extensive technical skills. The process of generating images involves straightforward text prompts, making it approachable for both beginners and seasoned creatives alike. This simplicity allows users to focus on their ideas and creativity rather than getting bogged down in complex software tools. As a result, individuals can experiment and iterate rapidly, fostering a more dynamic creative process.

Another advantage of Midjourney is its capacity for customization and versatility. Users can tweak their prompts to explore various styles, moods, and themes, resulting in a wide range of image outputs. This adaptability is particularly beneficial for content creators who need to maintain a consistent brand aesthetic or experiment with diverse visual approaches. Midjourney can generate everything from realistic landscapes to abstract art, allowing users to align their images closely with their project requirements, thus enhancing the overall quality and appeal of their work.

Midjourney fosters collaboration and community engagement among its users. The platform often features social elements where creators can share their generated images, gain inspiration from others, and receive feedback. This communal aspect not only encourages creativity but also helps users refine their skills and discover new techniques. For artists and graphic designers, networking with like-minded individuals can lead to fruitful collaborations and the exchange of ideas, further enriching their creative projects.

Utilizing Midjourney can save significant time and resources. Traditional image creation often involves lengthy processes, including brainstorming, sketching, and revisions. With Midjourney, users can rapidly generate multiple iterations of an image, allowing them to focus on refining their concepts instead of getting mired in the technicalities of design. This efficiency is particularly advantageous for bloggers and content creators who operate under tight deadlines or need to produce a high volume of visuals. By streamlining the image generation process, Midjourney empowers users to maximize their productivity while maintaining high standards of creativity.

Who Should Use Midjourney? - Define the target audience, including artists, designers, marketers, and hobbyists.

In the evolving landscape of digital creativity, Midjourney stands out as a powerful tool for image generation, catering to a diverse audience spanning various fields. Understanding who should utilize Midjourney is essential for maximizing its potential.

Artists, particularly those in visual disciplines, are among the most prominent users of Midjourney. With its ability to generate unique and intricate images from textual prompts, Midjourney offers artists a new medium to explore their ideas. Traditional methods can often be time-consuming and limiting, but by using Midjourney, artists can quickly visualize concepts and iterate on their work. This tool can serve as a source of inspiration, helping artists break through creative blocks and experiment with styles or themes that they may not have considered otherwise.

Graphic designers also find immense value in Midjourney. The platform allows designers to create high-quality visuals rapidly, making it an ideal resource for both personal projects and professional assignments. From generating eye-catching graphics for marketing campaigns to crafting custom illustrations for branding purposes, Midjourney can streamline the design process. Additionally, designers can utilize the generated images as a starting point, refining and adapting them to fit their specific needs, thus enhancing their efficiency and creativity in project execution.

Marketers represent another significant demographic that can benefit from Midjourney's capabilities. In an era where visual content is paramount for engaging audiences, marketers need tools that can keep up with the demand for fresh and compelling imagery. Midjourney can help marketers create unique visuals for social media posts, advertisements, and promotional materials, allowing them to maintain a consistent brand presence. By harnessing the power of AI-generated images, marketers can appeal to their target demographics more effectively while saving time and resources in the creative process.

Hobbyists and enthusiasts who enjoy exploring digital art and image generation can find a welcoming space in Midjourney. This group includes individuals who may not have formal training in art or design but are eager to express themselves creatively. Midjourney provides an accessible entry point for these users, allowing them to experiment with image generation without the steep learning curve often associated with traditional art techniques. Through engaging with Midjourney, hobbyists can develop their skills, gain confidence in their creative abilities, and even share their work with a broader community.

Midjourney caters to a wide range of users, including artists, graphic designers, marketers, and hobbyists. Each of these groups can leverage the platform's capabilities to enhance their creative processes, whether by generating new ideas, streamlining workflows, or creating unique visuals. Understanding the diverse target audience for Midjourney underscores its potential to transform how individuals and professionals approach image generation, making it an invaluable tool in the modern creative toolkit.

Chapter 2: Getting Started with Midjourney

How to Create a Midjourney Account

Creating a Midjourney account is an essential first step for anyone looking to explore the platform's powerful image generation capabilities. Whether you are a blogger, content creator, artist, or graphic designer, having an account allows you to access a variety of tools that can enhance your creative projects.

To begin, visit the official Midjourney website https://midjourney.com.

Here, you will find a prominent "Sign Up" button on the homepage. Click on this button to initiate the account creation process. You will be directed to a registration page where you will need to provide basic information such as your name, email address, and a secure password. It is important to choose a password that is both memorable and complex enough to protect your account. After filling in the required fields, make sure to read the terms of service and privacy policy, as understanding these documents is crucial for responsible usage of the platform.

Once you have completed the registration form, you will need to verify your email address. Check your inbox for a verification email from Midjourney. If you do not see it within a few minutes, check your spam or junk folder, as sometimes automated emails can end up there. Click on the verification link provided in the email to confirm your address. This step is vital, as it activates your account and allows you to proceed with the setup process.

After verifying your email, return to the Midjourney website and log in using the credentials you just created. Upon logging in for the first time, you may be prompted to fill out additional information, such as your profile preferences and interests. This information helps tailor your experience on the platform and allows Midjourney to recommend features and resources that align with your creative goals. Take your time to explore these settings, as they can significantly enhance your user experience.

Finally, familiarize yourself with the platform's interface. Midjourney offers a plethora of tools and resources designed to facilitate image generation. Spend some time navigating through the dashboard, checking out the tutorial sections, and exploring community forums where you can connect with other users. Understanding the layout will not only make it easier to use the platform but also inspire you to dive into the creative possibilities that Midjourney offers. With your account successfully set up, you are now ready to embark on your journey toward creating stunning images tailored to your unique vision.

Navigating the User Interface

Navigating the user interface of Midjourney is essential for anyone seeking to harness its powerful capabilities for image generation. The interface is designed to be intuitive, but understanding its various sections can significantly enhance the user experience.

The primary section of the Midjourney interface consists of the command input area. This is where users can enter text prompts that guide the AI in creating images. To make the most out of this feature, it is crucial to understand how to construct effective prompts. Users should start with a clear idea of what they want to visualize, using descriptive language that includes specific details about style, color, and subject matter. The command input area also allows for modifiers and parameters, enabling users to fine-tune their prompts further. Familiarizing oneself with these options opens up a broader spectrum of creative possibilities.

Adjacent to the command input area is the output display section, where generated images are showcased. This area is vital for reviewing the results of your prompts. Users can see how well the AI interpreted their requests and can easily cycle through multiple outputs generated from a single prompt. Understanding the layout of this section helps users quickly identify their preferred images for further refinement or sharing. It is advisable to take notes on what worked well and what didn't, as this can inform future prompt crafting, making the process more efficient over time.

Another important feature is the settings menu, which provides users with various customization options. In this section, users can adjust parameters such as aspect ratio, quality, and style presets. These settings allow for a more tailored approach to image generation. For instance, artists and graphic designers may prefer a higher quality setting to ensure that the details in their images are crisp and clear, while bloggers might choose a quicker generation time for timely content production. Experimenting with these settings can yield different artistic effects and help users discover their unique style.

The community interaction section enables users to connect with other Midjourney enthusiasts. This area often includes forums or chat features where users can share their creations, seek feedback, and exchange tips. Engaging with the community can provide valuable insights into new techniques and trends, enhancing the overall experience of using Midjourney. For content creators and artists, networking with peers can inspire collaboration and innovation, making the creative process even more enriching.

In summary, navigating the user interface of Midjourney involves understanding the command input area, output display, settings menu, and community interaction features. Each section plays a pivotal role in the image generation process, allowing users to optimize their experience and produce high-quality visuals. By breaking down these components and mastering their use, individuals can effectively unlock the full potential of Midjourney, transforming their concepts into captivating creations.

System Requirements

When considering the implementation of Midjourney for image generation, understanding the system requirements is paramount for ensuring a smooth and efficient user experience.

Starting with hardware requirements, a robust computer system is fundamental. Users should aim for a machine equipped with a modern multi-core processor, preferably from the latest generations of Intel or AMD. A minimum of 16 GB of RAM is recommended, as this allows for better multitasking and handling of larger image files, which are common in graphic design and content creation. Additionally, a dedicated graphics card with at least 4 GB of VRAM will significantly enhance the rendering performance of Midjourney. This is particularly vital for artists and graphic designers who may be working with complex images and requiring faster processing times.

On the software front, users need to ensure they have a compatible operating system. Midjourney runs smoothly on Windows 10 or higher, and macOS versions from Catalina onwards. Users should also have the latest version of a web browser, preferably Google Chrome or Mozilla Firefox, as Midjourney operates primarily through web-based platforms. Keeping the browser updated ensures that all functionalities are available and minimizes the risk of encountering bugs or compatibility issues during usage.

Internet connectivity is another crucial aspect to consider. Midjourney relies on cloud processing, meaning a stable and high-speed internet connection is essential for optimal performance. Users should aim for a broadband connection with at least 25 Mbps download speed to facilitate quick uploads and downloads of images. A reliable connection not only enhances the user experience but also significantly reduces the risk of interruptions during image generation, which can be particularly frustrating for content creators and artists working under tight deadlines.

Finally, users should consider auxiliary software that can complement their experience with Midjourney. Graphics editing software such as Adobe Photoshop or GIMP can be invaluable for post-processing images generated by Midjourney. Users may benefit from project management tools or digital asset management software to keep their creative work organized. By ensuring that both hardware and software are up to par, users will be well-equipped to harness the full potential of Midjourney, paving the way for innovative and high-quality image generation in their respective fields.

Subscription Plans

In the realm of image generation using Midjourney, understanding the various subscription plans available is crucial for maximizing the platform's potential. Midjourney offers a range of subscription options tailored to different user needs, from casual creators to professional artists. Each plan provides distinct features and limits on usage, making it essential to assess your requirements before committing to a subscription. By evaluating factors such as frequency of use, the complexity of projects, and budget, users can choose the most suitable plan that aligns with their creative goals.

Midjourney offers several subscription models to cater to different user needs. The main options typically include:

- **Basic Plan**: This plan usually provides a limited number of image generations per month, suitable for casual users or hobbyists.

- **Standard Plan**: Designed for more frequent users, this plan typically offers a higher limit on image generations and may include additional features such as faster processing times.

- **Pro Plan**: Aimed at professional users or businesses, this plan generally includes unlimited image generations, priority access to new features, and enhanced support.

- **Enterprise Plan**: This model is often customizable and tailored for large organizations, providing advanced features, dedicated support, and potentially the ability to integrate with other systems.

Each plan may come with specific benefits, such as access to higher resolution images, commercial usage rights, or exclusive content. It's advisable to check Midjourney's official website for the most current details, as offerings can change.

The basic subscription typically serves as an entry point for individuals who are new to image generation or those who need it for occasional projects. This plan usually includes a limited number of image generations per month and may restrict access to certain features or higher-resolution outputs. For bloggers and content creators who require images on a less frequent basis, this option provides an affordable way to experiment with Midjourney's capabilities without overwhelming financial commitment. It allows users to familiarize themselves with the platform while producing quality visuals for their blogs or social media.

For artists and graphic designers who engage in more frequent and intensive image generation, a higher-tier subscription may be more appropriate. These plans often include increased generation limits, access to advanced features, and priority support. This level of subscription is beneficial for professionals who need to produce a large volume of images or require high-resolution outputs for print or commercial use. By investing in a more comprehensive plan, users can ensure they have the resources needed to fulfill their creative visions without interruptions.

It is also important to consider the collaborative aspect of image generation when choosing a subscription. Some plans may offer features that facilitate teamwork, such as shared project spaces and collaborative tools. For content creators who work with teams, these features can enhance productivity and streamline the creative process. Evaluating the need for collaboration is a key factor in determining the best subscription plan, as it can significantly impact the efficiency and effectiveness of the image generation workflow.

Selecting the right subscription plan for Midjourney involves a careful assessment of individual needs and creative aspirations. Users should reflect on how often they anticipate generating images, the types of projects they plan to undertake, and any collaborative efforts they may engage in. By aligning the chosen plan with specific goals and budget constraints, users can unlock the full potential of Midjourney, transforming their concepts into compelling visual narratives. This thoughtful approach to subscription selection not only enhances the creative process but also ensures that each user can make the most of their investment in this powerful image generation tool.

Chapter 3: Fundamentals of AI Image Generation

What is AI-Powered Image Generation?

AI-powered image generation refers to the process of creating images using artificial intelligence algorithms. In simple terms, it's like teaching a computer to draw or paint by feeding it a vast amount of visual information. The AI learns from this data to understand and replicate various artistic styles, subjects, and compositions. As a result, users can generate unique images based on specific prompts or themes, allowing for endless creative possibilities. This technology is particularly valuable for bloggers, content creators, artists, and graphic designers looking to enhance their visual content without the need for extensive artistic skills.

The foundation of AI image generation lies in machine learning, a subset of artificial intelligence. In this process, the AI is trained on a massive dataset consisting of millions of images. During training, it analyzes various features such as color, texture, shape, and composition. By understanding these elements, the AI develops a model that can generate new images that reflect the learned styles and characteristics. This training phase is crucial, as the quality and diversity of the dataset directly influence the AI's ability to create compelling images.

Once the AI model is trained, it can generate images based on textual prompts provided by users. For example, if a user inputs a description like "a serene landscape with mountains and a sunset," the AI interprets the prompt and synthesizes an image that embodies those elements. This process typically involves a complex interplay of algorithms that translate written language into visual representation. The result is a unique image that can serve various purposes, from enhancing blog posts to inspiring graphic design projects.

AI-powered image generation tools, such as Midjourney, offer user-friendly interfaces that allow individuals with varying levels of technical expertise to create stunning visuals. Users can experiment with different prompts, styles, and settings to refine their images. The accessibility of these tools democratizes the creative process, enabling anyone—from hobbyists to professionals—to produce high-quality images quickly. This ease of use is particularly beneficial for content creators who need to generate engaging visuals on tight deadlines.

AI-powered image generation is a transformative technology that combines machine learning with creative expression. By understanding how AI interprets and generates images, users can leverage tools like Midjourney to enhance their projects and explore new artistic avenues. As this technology continues to evolve, it opens up exciting possibilities for bloggers, artists, and designers, allowing them to focus more on their ideas and concepts while leaving the intricate details of image creation to the AI.

Key Terminology in Midjourney

In the realm of Midjourney image generation, understanding key terminology is crucial for effectively navigating the platform.

The term "prompt" is foundational in the Midjourney ecosystem. A prompt is essentially a textual input that you provide to the system to guide the image generation process. It serves as a creative seed from which the AI will draw inspiration and create visuals. Crafting a well-structured prompt involves being specific about the elements you want to see in the image, such as colors, themes, and styles. For instance, instead of simply typing "cat," a more effective prompt might be "a fluffy orange cat lounging on a sunny windowsill." This specificity helps the AI better understand your vision and translate it into a unique image.

"Iteration" refers to the process of refining and improving an image through multiple rounds of generation based on feedback or new ideas. In the context of Midjourney, iteration allows users to explore different interpretations of their prompts or make adjustments to achieve a desired outcome. After generating an initial image, you may decide to tweak your prompt or adjust certain details, resulting in a new version that aligns more closely with your artistic vision. Embracing iteration is key to honing your skills as an image creator, as it encourages experimentation and fosters a deeper understanding of how the AI interprets prompts.

Parameters play a vital role in customizing the image generation process. In Midjourney, parameters are specific settings or modifiers that influence how the AI interprets your prompt and generates images. These can include aspects such as style, resolution, and aspect ratio, among others. By adjusting parameters, users can tailor their images to fit specific needs or aesthetics. For example, if you're a graphic designer looking for a particular style, you might use parameters to dictate that the generated image should have a minimalistic design or vibrant color palette. Learning how to effectively use parameters allows for greater control and creativity in your image-making endeavors.

Understanding these key terms—prompt, iteration, and parameters—equips users with the language and tools needed to navigate Midjourney confidently. As you embark on your journey of image generation, remember that these concepts are interconnected. A well-crafted prompt can lead to productive iterations, and the right parameters can enhance the final output. By mastering these terms, you will not only improve your image generation skills but also unlock the full potential of Midjourney, enabling you to create stunning visuals that resonate with your audience.

How Midjourney Works

Midjourney operates as a cutting-edge artificial intelligence tool designed specifically for generating images based on user-provided prompts. The process begins when users input a textual description or idea into the platform. This prompt serves as the foundation for the AI's creative interpretation. The clarity and specificity of the prompt significantly influence the quality and relevance of the generated image. Users can experiment with different phrasing, adjectives, and themes to guide the AI toward producing images that align with their vision. This initial step is crucial, as it sets the stage for the entire image generation process.

Once a prompt is submitted, Midjourney utilizes a sophisticated model trained on a vast dataset of images and corresponding textual descriptions. The AI analyzes the input to identify key elements, such as objects, colors, styles, and emotions, which it then combines in unique ways. This process involves complex algorithms that allow the AI to draw from its extensive knowledge base, effectively translating the textual input into visual representations. As a result, users can receive images that capture not only the literal aspects of their prompts but also the underlying themes and nuances.

The image generation process typically takes place in a matter of seconds, showcasing the power of modern machine learning techniques. Midjourney employs a neural network architecture that iteratively refines its output. Initially, a rough draft of the image is created, which is then refined through multiple iterations. Each cycle enhances the image's details, colors, and overall composition, enabling the AI to create visually compelling and coherent images that resonate with the user's intent. This iterative refinement process is a key feature that distinguishes Midjourney from other image generation tools.

Midjourney allows for user interaction and feedback during the image creation process. After the initial image is generated, users can provide additional prompts or make adjustments to refine the image further. This interactive element enables users to experiment and explore various artistic directions without being confined to their original input. For content creators, artists, and graphic designers, this flexibility is invaluable, as it opens up avenues for creativity and innovation that can enhance their projects and visual storytelling.

Midjourney combines advanced AI technology with user-driven input to create a dynamic image generation experience. By carefully crafting prompts and engaging with the AI throughout the process, users can harness the full potential of this tool. Whether for personal projects, blog illustrations, or professional artwork, understanding how Midjourney interprets and visualizes prompts is essential for anyone looking to leverage this powerful resource in their creative endeavors.

What Does /imagine Mean in Midjourney?

In Midjourney, the command "/imagine" is used to prompt the AI to generate images based on a user's description. Users can input specific details, themes, styles, or elements they want to see in the artwork, and the AI will interpret these prompts to create unique visual representations. This feature allows for a high degree of creativity and customization, enabling users to explore various artistic concepts and ideas through generated imagery. Users can experiment with different parameters, such as color schemes, styles, and subjects, allowing them to see how minor adjustments can lead to vastly different artistic outcomes.

How to Create your First Image with the /imagine Command

To create your first image in Midjourney, follow these steps:

1. **Join the Midjourney Discord Server**: If you haven't done so yet, I recommend that you begin by joining the Midjourney server on Discord. You can easily find the invitation link by visiting the Midjourney website.

2. **Find a Bot Channel**: Once you have successfully joined the server, take a moment to look for channels specifically designated for bot commands. These are typically labeled with names like `#newbies`, `#bot-commands`, or something comparable. If you are unfamiliar with the platform, beginning your journey in a channel meant for newcomers is highly advisable and can help you get oriented.

3. **Activate the /imagine Command**: In the chat input box, enter the command `/imagine` followed by a space. This action effectively prompts the bot to get ready and prepare itself for the input you are about to provide next.

4. **Describe Your Image**: After entering `/imagine`, provide a detailed description of the image you wish to create. Be specific about the elements you want, including colors, styles, subjects, and mood. For instance, you might write `/imagine a peaceful landscape with mountains at sunset and a clear lake`.

5. **Submit the Command**: Once your description is complete, press Enter to send the command. The Midjourney bot will process your request.

6. **Wait for the Image**: The bot will take a moment to generate your image. You will see a notification indicating that the image is being created, followed by the bot posting the generated image in the channel.

7. **Review and Refine**: After the image is generated, take a moment to review it. If you'd like to make adjustments or explore a different idea, modify your description and use the `/imagine` command again.

8. **Save or Share Your Image**: If you're satisfied with the result, click on the image to view it in full size, then save it to your device or share it as desired.re it as needed.

By following these steps, you'll be able to create unique images using Midjourney's powerful AI capabilities in Discord.

Variation and Upscale in Midjourney

The Variation and Upscale buttons play crucial roles in enhancing user creativity and refining generated images. The Variation button allows users to create alternative versions of an image, offering different interpretations or styles based on the original prompt. This feature encourages experimentation, enabling artists to explore diverse aesthetics and ideas. On the other hand, the Upscale button enhances the resolution of a selected image, providing greater detail and clarity. This is particularly valuable for users who wish to produce high-quality visuals suitable for various applications, from digital art to print. Together, these tools empower users to refine their artistic visions and achieve the desired visual impact.

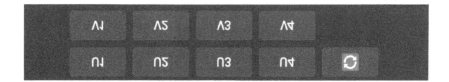

U buttons upscale the selected image

- V buttions create slight variations of the selected image
- and the □ button reruns a Job

Chapter 4: Writing Effective Prompts

Why Prompts Matter

Clear and descriptive prompts are the cornerstone of successful image generation in Midjourney, serving as the bridge between the creator's vision and the algorithm's interpretation. When users provide specific prompts, they significantly enhance the likelihood of generating images that align with their expectations. A well-crafted prompt acts as a guiding thread, directing the AI to understand not just the subject matter but also the mood, style, and intricate details that the creator envisions. This clarity is paramount, especially for those new to the platform, as it can dramatically reduce the gap between concept and execution.

The significance of prompts extends beyond mere clarity; they are also essential for capturing nuances that breathe life into generated images. A vague or ambiguous prompt might lead to outputs that are uninspired or far removed from the creator's intent. In contrast, descriptive prompts can encapsulate specific elements such as color schemes, artistic styles, and even the emotional tone of the desired image. For instance, instead of simply requesting "a landscape," a more effective prompt would describe "a serene sunset over a tranquil lake surrounded by vibrant autumn foliage." This level of detail invites the AI to produce an image that resonates more closely with the user's vision.

The iterative nature of image generation in Midjourney emphasizes the importance of prompt refinement. With each round of generation, users can analyze the output and adjust their prompts accordingly, honing in on the desired result. This process not only fosters a deeper understanding of how the AI interprets language but also empowers users to experiment with different descriptive techniques. As creators gain experience, they learn how subtle shifts in wording can lead to significantly varied outputs, thereby enhancing their ability to convey complex ideas through prompts.

In a landscape where visual content is paramount for engagement, especially for bloggers, content creators, and graphic designers, the ability to generate compelling images is invaluable. Well-structured prompts allow these individuals to maintain their unique voice and style while leveraging AI technology to produce high-quality visuals. By investing time in crafting precise prompts, creators can ensure their images not only capture attention but also effectively communicate their intended messages. This synergy between human creativity and AI capabilities can result in content that is not only visually appealing but also rich in narrative depth.

Understanding the importance of prompts cultivates a more constructive relationship between the user and the tool. As creators become adept at formulating effective prompts, they unlock the full potential of Midjourney, transforming it from a mere image generation tool into a collaborative partner in the creative process. The journey from concept to creation is thus enriched, as users learn to articulate their ideas more clearly and engage more meaningfully with the technology at their disposal. In this way, the art of prompt writing becomes a fundamental skill that enhances both the efficiency and the quality of image generation, paving the way for innovation and inspiration in the digital realm.

Types of Prompts: Descriptive vs. Abstract

In the realm of image generation with Midjourney, understanding the types of prompts used can significantly impact the outcome of your creative projects. Two primary categories of prompts are descriptive and abstract. Each type serves its own purpose and can lead to distinct stylistic interpretations in the generated images. By recognizing the differences between these prompt types, users can tailor their approaches to achieve their desired results, particularly when exploring the capabilities of Midjourney.

Descriptive prompts are characterized by their specificity and detail. They provide clear, tangible information about the subject matter, which guides the image generation process toward producing recognizable and concrete visuals. For instance, a descriptive prompt might read, "A serene landscape featuring a vibrant sunset over a calm lake, with mountains in the background and a silhouette of a lone boat floating." This prompt paints a vivid picture, allowing Midjourney to generate an image that captures the essence of the described scene. When using descriptive prompts, it's beneficial to include sensory details, such as colors, textures, and specific elements, to enhance the clarity of the generated image.

In contrast, abstract prompts are more open-ended and often rely on themes, emotions, or conceptual ideas rather than concrete imagery. For example, an abstract prompt could be "The feeling of nostalgia expressed through swirling colors and blurred shapes." This type of prompt allows for greater artistic freedom, inviting Midjourney to explore interpretations that may not be immediately recognizable but evoke a certain mood or atmosphere. Abstract prompts are particularly useful when the goal is to provoke thought, inspire creative exploration, or convey complex emotional states without the constraints of realistic representation.

When deciding between descriptive and abstract prompts, consider the intent behind your image generation. If the objective is to create a clear representation of a specific idea or scene, descriptive prompts are the way to go. They are ideal for projects requiring precision, such as illustrations for blogs, articles, or graphic design work where the audience needs to understand the visual context clearly. Conversely, if you aim to provoke emotion or explore a conceptual theme, abstract prompts can offer a richer, more nuanced outcome. They are often used in artistic endeavors where the focus is on evoking feelings or stimulating imagination rather than depicting a specific scene.

The choice between descriptive and abstract prompts hinges on the desired outcome and the audience's needs. By experimenting with both types, users can gain a deeper understanding of how Midjourney interprets prompts and the kinds of images each can generate. This knowledge not only enhances the creative process but also empowers content creators, artists, and graphic designers to harness the full potential of Midjourney, transforming their concepts into compelling visual narratives.

How to Write Compelling Prompts

Crafting effective prompts is crucial for generating high-quality images in Midjourney. A well-structured prompt serves as the foundation for the creative output you desire. Start by clearly defining the subject of your image. Whether you're aiming for a serene landscape, a bustling urban scene, or a whimsical character, specificity in your subject will guide the AI in producing more focused and meaningful visuals. Instead of vague descriptors, use precise language that captures the essence of what you envision. For instance, rather than simply stating "a tree," consider "a majestic oak tree in the golden light of sunset," which provides a clearer context for the AI to work with.

In addition to defining your subject, the inclusion of adjectives can significantly enhance the richness of your prompt. Descriptive adjectives convey your intended mood, style, and atmosphere, shaping the way the image comes to life. Words like "vibrant," "mysterious," or "tranquil" help to set the emotional tone and influence the visual palette. Consider incorporating sensory details that evoke a more immersive experience. For example, instead of just "a beach," you might describe "a sun-kissed beach with soft white sand, lapping waves, and a vibrant sunset." This level of detail not only enriches the prompt but also allows the AI to generate images that resonate more deeply.

The structure of your prompt also plays a pivotal role in its effectiveness. A well-organized prompt typically follows a pattern that starts with the subject, followed by adjectives, and concludes with additional context or settings. For instance, "A vintage bicycle (subject) in a lush green park (context), surrounded by blooming flowers (additional detail)." This structure helps the AI prioritize the elements you consider most important and ensures that the generated image aligns closely with your vision. By maintaining clarity and logical progression in your prompt, you can improve the coherence of the resulting images.

Word choice is another critical aspect of prompt creation. The vocabulary you use can drastically alter the interpretations made by the AI. Opt for strong, evocative words that carry specific connotations. For example, instead of saying "a building," you might say "a crumbling Gothic cathedral," which paints a more vivid picture. Avoid generic terms that might lead to ambiguity; instead, select words that convey particular characteristics or emotions. This attention to language not only enhances the quality of the image but also ensures that it aligns more closely with your creative intent.

Experimentation is key in the process of crafting compelling prompts. Don't hesitate to iterate on your initial ideas. Test different combinations of words, structures, and contexts to discover what resonates best with your artistic vision. Keep a record of successful prompts and their corresponding images to refine your approach over time. Learning how the AI interprets various descriptors will empower you to create more precise and engaging prompts. By embracing both the art and science of prompt crafting, you can unlock the full potential of Midjourney, resulting in stunning visuals that elevate your projects, blogs, or artistic endeavors.

Chapter 5: Exploring Midjourney's Features

Customizing Image Styles and Themes

Customizing image styles and themes is an essential aspect of using Midjourney to bring creative visions to life. As users delve into the platform, they discover a range of tools and options that enable them to fine-tune their images to better align with their artistic intentions.

One of the first steps in customizing image styles is understanding the various options available within Midjourney. The platform provides predefined styles that can be easily applied to images, each reflecting different artistic movements or techniques. For instance, users can explore styles reminiscent of impressionism, surrealism, or even contemporary digital art. These predefined styles serve as starting points, allowing users to select a foundation that aligns closely with their creative goals. By experimenting with different styles, users can quickly identify what resonates with their vision while gaining insights into the potential of Midjourney's capabilities.

In addition to predefined styles, Midjourney offers flexibility through customizable parameters. Users can adjust various settings, such as color palettes, textures, and lighting effects, to create a more personalized image. For instance, by modifying the color scheme to incorporate specific shades that reflect a brand identity or a thematic element of a blog post, users can achieve a cohesive look that enhances storytelling. Experimenting with different combinations of these parameters can lead to unexpected and compelling results, further enriching the creative process.

Themes play a critical role in the visual narrative of an image. Users can establish a theme by focusing on specific subjects, moods, or concepts that they want to convey. Midjourney allows users to infuse their images with thematic elements by inputting descriptive prompts that encapsulate their desired atmosphere or message. For example, if a user aims to create an image that evokes tranquility, they can incorporate keywords such as "calm," "serene," or "natural" into their prompts. This ability to weave in thematic elements not only enhances the overall impact of the image but also ensures that it aligns with the broader context of the user's content.

Collaboration and feedback are vital components of the customization process. Users, especially those in creative fields, can benefit from sharing their Midjourney-generated images with peers or audiences to gather insights and suggestions. This collaborative approach can lead to new ideas for adjustments in style or theme that may not have been initially considered. Engaging with a community of fellow content creators, artists, and designers can foster an environment of creativity where users can learn from each other's experiences and refine their own image generation techniques.

Customizing image styles and themes in Midjourney is a powerful way for users to align their generated images with their creative goals. By utilizing predefined styles, adjusting customizable parameters, establishing thematic elements, and engaging with a community for feedback, users can elevate their image generation experience. The ability to tailor images according to personal or project-specific needs not only enhances artistic expression but also empowers users to produce captivating visuals that resonate with their intended audience.

Mastering Aspect Ratios

Mastering aspect ratios is a crucial aspect of image generation that can significantly influence the composition and overall impact of your visuals. An aspect ratio is defined as the proportional relationship between the width and height of an image. Typically expressed as two numbers separated by a colon (e.g., 16:9), the first number represents the width, while the second indicates the height. Understanding aspect ratios is essential for content creators, as they determine how an image will be displayed across various platforms, affecting both aesthetics and functionality.

Different aspect ratios serve distinct purposes and can create varied visual experiences. Common ratios include 1:1 (square), 4:3 (standard), 16:9 (widescreen), and 2:1 (panoramic). The square aspect ratio is often favored for social media posts, as it occupies more screen space on mobile devices, making images more engaging. In contrast, the 16:9 ratio is prevalent in video and cinematic contexts, providing a broader field of view that enhances storytelling. By selecting the appropriate aspect ratio, creators can tailor their images to the intended audience and platform, ensuring maximum visual impact.

When using Midjourney, the choice of aspect ratio can dramatically alter the perception of your generated images. For instance, a landscape-oriented image may evoke a sense of expansiveness and tranquility, while a portrait-oriented image often emphasizes subjects and details, creating a more intimate atmosphere. Additionally, experimenting with less common ratios, such as 2:1 or even 21:9, can produce striking visuals that stand out in a crowded digital space. This flexibility allows creators to push the boundaries of traditional compositions and explore new creative avenues.

It is also important to consider how different aspect ratios affect the framing and focal points within an image. A wider aspect ratio can accommodate more elements within the frame, inviting viewers to explore the composition more deeply. Conversely, a narrower aspect ratio may force a tighter focus on a specific subject, enhancing its prominence and drawing attention to finer details. Understanding these dynamics will empower creators to make deliberate choices that align with their artistic vision and narrative goals.

You can define the aspect ratio with a 'parameter' called --aspect or --ar. More on parameters in the next chapter. For example, you'd write your prompt, followed by "--aspect <3:2>" for an image that has an aspect ratio of 3x2 (width, then height). That's a typical horizontal photograph.

Using Parameters to Enhance Results

Midjourney provides a variety of parameters that allow users to fine-tune their image generation process, enhancing the control and specific outcomes for creative projects. Here are some key parameters to be familiar with:

1. **--aspect <width:height> or --ar**: This parameter changes the aspect ratio of the generated image. For example, using `--ar 16:9` will produce a landscape-oriented image, while `--ar 9:16` will yield a portrait-oriented image. Adjusting the aspect ratio can significantly impact the composition and feel of the image.

2. **--chaos <number 0–100>**: This parameter controls the level of randomness and uniqueness in the generated images. A

lower value (e.g., 0-20) will produce more consistent and predictable results, while a higher value (e.g., 80-100) encourages more variability and creativity in the outputs. This is useful for users looking to explore diverse interpretations of a prompt.

3. **--style <4a, 4b, or 4c>**: This parameter allows users to select between different versions of Midjourney's model 4. Each style offers distinct characteristics and rendering approaches, enabling users to choose the one that best fits their artistic vision or project requirements.

4. **--niji**: This parameter activates an alternative model specifically designed for generating anime-style images. Using `--niji` can yield results that are more aligned with anime aesthetics, making it ideal for projects focused on that genre.

5. **--quality <.25, .5, 1, or 2> or --q <.25, .5, 1, or 2>**: This parameter controls the amount of rendering quality time allocated to the image generation. Higher values result in more detailed and refined images but may take longer to process. For example, `--q 2` will provide the highest quality output, while `--q .25` will generate images more quickly but with lower detail.

These parameters empower users to tailor their image generation experience, allowing for greater precision in achieving desired artistic outcomes. By adjusting these settings, users can effectively navigate the balance between creativity, quality, and specific stylistic choices in their projects.

Then, there is the **--v** parameter, which stands for version, allows users to specify which iteration of the Midjourney algorithm they wish to utilize for their image generation. This is particularly beneficial as different versions may incorporate various improvements, features, or stylistic tendencies. For example, the latest version might produce more detailed images or offer enhanced capabilities for specific styles. By experimenting with different versions, users can discover which one aligns best with their creative vision, thereby optimizing the quality and relevance of the generated images.

Utilizing these parameters effectively requires a thoughtful approach to the image creation process. For instance, a content creator aiming to produce visually striking blog graphics might decide to use the --ar parameter to create a 16:9 aspect ratio, ideal for website banners. Simultaneously, they could experiment with different versions to see which one yields the most vibrant colors or intricate details that align with their brand's identity. This strategic use of parameters elevates the creative process from mere image generation to a more deliberate and impactful form of visual storytelling.

Furthermore, mastering these parameters encourages a deeper understanding of Midjourney's capabilities and the nuances of digital art. As users grow more familiar with how different parameters affect their results, they can begin to innovate and push the boundaries of what is possible within the platform. This exploration fosters creativity and allows artists, graphic designers, and content creators to produce unique images that stand out in a crowded digital landscape. Ultimately, leveraging parameters like --v and --ar is not just about technical proficiency; it's about enhancing artistic expression and achieving a more refined visual output that resonates with audiences.

Chapter 6: Techniques for Image Generation

Beginner-Friendly Techniques

In the realm of image generation, particularly with Midjourney, beginners may feel overwhelmed by the myriad of possibilities at their fingertips. However, the process can be simplified by employing a set of beginner-friendly techniques that facilitate high-quality image creation. Understanding these fundamental strategies will empower users to navigate the platform with confidence and creativity, unlocking their potential as content creators, artists, or graphic designers.

One of the most effective techniques for new users is the practice of utilizing clear and descriptive prompts. The beauty of Midjourney lies in its ability to interpret and visualize written instructions. Beginners should focus on crafting prompts that include specific adjectives, styles, and subjects. For instance, rather than simply stating "a landscape," a more detailed prompt like "a serene sunset over a tranquil lake with mountains in the background" provides the AI with a clearer direction. By honing the skill of prompt-writing, users can significantly enhance the quality of the images generated.

Another beginner-friendly technique is to leverage reference images. Midjourney allows users to upload examples that reflect the desired outcome or style. This feature is particularly valuable for those who may struggle to articulate their vision through text alone. By providing a reference image, users can guide the AI toward a specific aesthetic or theme, ensuring that the generated images align more closely with their expectations. This approach not only simplifies the process but also serves as a useful learning tool for understanding how different elements contribute to a cohesive visual narrative.

Experimentation is key in the journey of mastering Midjourney. Beginners should feel encouraged to try different combinations of styles, subjects, and techniques. By varying their prompts and reference images, users can discover what resonates with their personal artistic vision. This trial-and-error approach often leads to unexpected and delightful results, fostering a sense of creativity and exploration. It is essential for beginners to remember that every generated image, regardless of its quality, serves as an opportunity for learning and growth.

Taking advantage of community resources can significantly enhance the learning experience. Midjourney has a vibrant community where users share their experiences, tips, and tricks. Engaging with fellow creators through forums, social media, or dedicated groups can provide invaluable insights and inspiration. Observing the techniques used by others can spark new ideas and encourage users to push their creative boundaries. Collaboration and feedback from the community can also help beginners refine their skills and gain confidence in their image generation process.

Finally, understanding the importance of post-processing can elevate the quality of images generated in Midjourney. Beginners should explore basic editing tools available in photo editing software to enhance their images further. Simple adjustments such as brightness, contrast, and color saturation can make a significant difference in the final presentation. By combining the strengths of Midjourney's image generation capabilities with post-processing techniques, users can create visually stunning and polished images that are ready for sharing or publication. Through these beginner-friendly techniques, individuals can embark on a fulfilling journey of creativity and expression using Midjourney.

Intermediate and Advanced Techniques

Intermediate and advanced techniques in Midjourney allow experienced users to unlock a higher level of creativity and precision in their image generation process. As you grow more comfortable with basic image generation techniques, it becomes essential to explore more complex strategies that can enhance your creative output.

Chaining prompts is a powerful technique that involves linking multiple prompts together to build upon previous outputs. This iterative approach allows you to develop a more comprehensive image by refining specific aspects with each new prompt. For instance, you might start with a broad idea and generate an initial image, then create a follow-up prompt that specifies certain elements—like color schemes, styles, or additional subjects—to enhance or modify the original output. By employing this method, users can systematically explore variations and discover unique combinations that may not have emerged from a single prompt alone.

In addition to chaining prompts, leveraging advanced parameters can significantly elevate your image generation capabilities. Midjourney provides a range of parameters that allow you to control various aspects of the output, such as aspect ratio, quality, and stylization. By experimenting with parameters like `--ar` for aspect ratio adjustments or `--q` for quality settings, you can tailor your images to fit specific requirements or preferences. Understanding and applying these parameters will empower you to create images that are not only visually stunning but also suited to the intended application, whether that be a blog post, social media content, or a professional portfolio.

Another advanced technique to consider is the use of negative prompts, which allow you to specify what you do not want in your generated images. This can help refine the output by eliminating unwanted elements or styles that may detract from your vision. For example, if you're aiming for a serene landscape but want to avoid any urban features, incorporating a negative prompt can help guide Midjourney to focus solely on the natural aspects you desire. This targeted approach can save time and enhance the alignment of the generated images with your artistic goals.

Combining these techniques can lead to even more sophisticated results. By chaining prompts while simultaneously adjusting advanced parameters and using negative prompts, you can create a highly customized workflow. This level of control not only allows for greater creativity but also encourages experimentation. As you become more adept at using these intermediate and advanced techniques, you will find that your ability to generate compelling, high-quality images with Midjourney will flourish, paving the way for a more fulfilling creative journey.

Experimentation and Iteration

Experimentation and iteration are integral components of the creative process, especially when utilizing tools like Midjourney for image generation. By fostering a mindset that encourages experimentation, users can unlock new avenues of creativity and discover unexpected results. The iterative nature of working with image prompts allows creators to refine their ideas progressively, leading to enhanced outcomes that align more closely with their artistic vision.

One of the most effective ways to experiment with Midjourney is by varying the specificity of prompts. For instance, consider an initial prompt like "a serene landscape." While this may yield pleasant results, adjusting the prompt to include specific elements such as "a serene landscape with a glowing sunset, a calm lake reflecting the colors of the sky, and silhouettes of pine trees" can dramatically transform the output. The more detailed and vivid the prompt, the more likely it is to inspire the AI to generate a compelling and unique image. This demonstrates how slight modifications can lead to richer, more engaging visuals.

Another valuable technique involves altering the mood or style of the prompt. For example, if a creator begins with a straightforward prompt like "a city skyline," they might find it beneficial to experiment with various artistic styles or emotional tones. By rephrasing the prompt to "a dystopian city skyline at twilight, with dark clouds looming overhead and neon lights flickering," the resulting images might evoke a completely different atmosphere and narrative. This shift not only showcases the versatility of Midjourney but also encourages users to think critically about the emotions and themes they wish to convey through their images.

In addition to adjusting descriptive elements, experimenting with the structure of prompts can yield interesting results. Users might begin with a single, coherent prompt but can enhance their creativity by breaking it down into a list of keywords or phrases. For instance, instead of saying "a cozy café," one could list "cozy, café, warm lights, steaming coffee, people chatting." This method allows the AI to interpret the components individually, potentially resulting in a more dynamic composition. The key takeaway here is that by restructuring how prompts are presented, creators can facilitate richer interactions with the AI and discover images that resonate more profoundly with their artistic intent.

Embracing iteration is crucial in honing the image generation process. After generating an initial set of images, creators should not hesitate to revisit their prompts and make adjustments based on the outputs they receive. For example, if an image generated from a prompt is nearly perfect but lacks a particular detail, such as the presence of a character or an additional color palette, refining the prompt to include these elements can lead to a more satisfying final product. This iterative feedback loop encourages a deeper understanding of how the AI interprets various inputs, ultimately enhancing the user's ability to communicate their vision effectively.

Encouraging experimentation and iteration in the use of Midjourney not only fosters creativity but also empowers users to take ownership of their artistic journey. By adjusting prompts, exploring different styles, altering structures, and continuously refining their approach, creators can achieve remarkable breakthroughs in their image generation endeavors. This process is not just about producing visually appealing images; it's about cultivating a mindset that values exploration and growth, which is essential for any artist or designer looking to make their mark in the digital landscape.

Chapter 7: Best Practices for Creators

Ethics in AI Image Generation

Ethics in AI image generation has become an increasingly prominent topic, particularly as technologies like Midjourney gain traction among content creators, artists, and graphic designers. As users embrace the capabilities of AI to produce stunning visuals, it is essential to address the ethical implications that accompany this innovation. One of the primary concerns is the potential bias inherent in AI systems, which can inadvertently perpetuate stereotypes or misrepresent certain groups. Understanding these biases is crucial for anyone involved in image generation, as it allows creators to engage with their tools more thoughtfully and responsibly.

AI systems, including those used for image generation, learn from vast datasets that may contain historical biases or unbalanced representations. For instance, if a model is trained predominantly on images featuring certain demographics, the output may reflect a skewed perspective that excludes or misrepresents others. This can result in artwork that reinforces harmful stereotypes or fails to represent the diversity of human experience. For individuals working with Midjourney, being aware of these biases is the first step toward mitigating their impact and ensuring that generated content is inclusive and representative of varied identities and cultures.

Another ethical concern revolves around the responsible use of generated content. As AI-generated images become more prevalent, the line between original creation and machine-generated art can blur, raising questions about authorship and ownership. Content creators must navigate these complexities carefully, considering how they attribute their work, especially if it incorporates AI-generated elements. It is vital to foster transparency in the creative process, ensuring audiences understand when an image has been generated or altered by AI and the extent of that involvement.

The potential for misuse of AI-generated images presents significant ethical challenges. From deepfakes to misleading representations in media, the technology can be exploited to create content that distorts reality or spreads misinformation. As users of Midjourney, creators bear a responsibility to use the tool ethically, ensuring that their images do not contribute to the proliferation of disinformation or unjust portrayals. Adopting a conscientious approach to how images are shared and utilized can help maintain the integrity of the digital landscape.

Engaging with AI image generation tools like Midjourney requires a commitment to ethical practices. By recognizing and addressing biases, understanding the implications of authorship, and committing to responsible usage, content creators can harness the power of AI while upholding the values of inclusivity and integrity. As the technology continues to evolve, fostering a culture of ethical mindfulness will be essential for ensuring that AI-generated content enriches rather than detracts from the creative community.

Copyright and Licensing

Understanding copyright laws is essential for anyone engaging with image generation, especially through platforms like Midjourney. Copyright is a legal framework that grants creators exclusive rights to their original works, including images, music, and text. This protection allows creators to control how their works are used and shared, which is crucial in a digital landscape where content can be easily reproduced and disseminated. For bloggers, content creators, artists, and graphic designers, having a clear grasp of copyright laws not only helps in avoiding potential legal issues but also empowers them to leverage their creations effectively.

When it comes to generated images, the copyright landscape can be complex. Generally, the creator of an original work holds the copyright, but the rules can differ based on the medium and the specific agreements in place. In the case of AI-generated images, like those produced by Midjourney, the copyright ownership may not be as straightforward. It's important to understand that while the AI facilitates the creation process, the human input—such as the prompts and settings used—plays a significant role in determining the originality of the output. Therefore, creators should familiarize themselves with the nuances of copyright as it applies to AI-generated content, which can sometimes be a gray area.

Midjourney has specific licensing policies in place that dictate how users can utilize the images generated on their platform. Understanding these policies is crucial for users who wish to incorporate these images into their work, whether for commercial or personal use. Midjourney typically offers various tiers of access, each with distinct licensing rights. For instance, some plans may allow for commercial use of generated images, while others might restrict usage to personal projects. Before embarking on a creative endeavor, it is essential to review the licensing agreements to ensure compliance and to understand the limitations that may affect how the images can be shared or sold.

In addition to individual licensing agreements, users should also be aware of the broader implications of using AI-generated images in their work. This includes potential issues related to derivative works and the ethical considerations of using AI for creative purposes. For instance, if Midjourney generates an image that closely resembles an existing copyrighted work, questions may arise about the originality of that image. Creators need to remain vigilant and ensure that their use of generated images does not infringe on the rights of others, thereby maintaining the integrity of their own work and avoiding legal complications.

Ultimately, navigating copyright laws and Midjourney's licensing policies requires diligence and a proactive approach. Creators should take the time to educate themselves about intellectual property rights, explore the specifics of Midjourney's agreements, and consider the broader implications of their work. By doing so, they can confidently utilize AI-generated images in a way that enhances their creative projects while respecting the rights of other creators. This understanding not only enriches the creative process but also fosters a more responsible and informed community of content creators.

Integrating Midjourney into Your Creative Workflow

Integrating Midjourney into your creative workflow can significantly enhance your content creation process, allowing for a seamless blend of AI-generated imagery and traditional artistic methods. The first step in this integration is to familiarize yourself with Midjourney's capabilities and features. Understand how to generate images that align with your vision by experimenting with prompts and settings. This exploratory phase is essential, as it will help you develop a sense of what types of images work best for your projects. By incorporating AI-generated images into your toolkit, you can save time on initial drafts and focus more on refining your concepts.

Once you have a grasp of Midjourney's functionalities, consider how to incorporate these images into your content effectively. For instance, if you are a blogger, think about using AI-generated visuals to accompany your written content. This could mean creating illustrations for articles, developing unique header images, or even generating background visuals for video content. The key is to ensure that the images resonate with your audience and enhance the overall message you want to convey. By strategically placing AI-generated images throughout your content, you can create a more engaging and visually appealing experience for your viewers.

Editing plays a crucial role in the integration of AI-generated images into your workflow. After generating images with Midjourney, it is essential to refine them to fit your specific needs and aesthetic preferences. Utilize graphic design software to adjust colors, crop images, or overlay text and graphics. This step allows you to personalize the AI-generated images and ensure they align with your branding. For artists and graphic designers, this editing phase may also involve combining AI outputs with traditional artwork or photographs, creating a hybrid approach that showcases your unique style.

Collaboration is another vital aspect of incorporating Midjourney into your creative workflow. If you work with a team—be it fellow bloggers, content creators, or graphic designers—consider using shared platforms that allow for easy access and feedback on AI-generated images. Tools like cloud storage or project management software can facilitate collaboration, enabling team members to view, comment on, and edit images collectively. This not only streamlines the creative process but also fosters a sense of community and shared vision among collaborators, leading to enhanced creativity and innovation.

As you continue to integrate Midjourney into your workflow, it's important to stay abreast of the latest developments in AI image generation. Follow updates from Midjourney and participate in community forums to learn from other users' experiences. By sharing tips and techniques, you can further refine your approach and discover new ways to utilize AI-generated images in your projects. Embracing an iterative mindset will allow you to adapt and evolve your creative practices, ensuring that the integration of AI remains a dynamic and enriching aspect of your content creation journey.

Chapter 8: Real-World Applications and Case Studies

How Bloggers Use Midjourney

Bloggers are increasingly turning to AI-generated visuals to enhance their content, and Midjourney stands out as a powerful tool in this realm. By leveraging Midjourney's capabilities, bloggers can create unique images that resonate with their audience, elevate the aesthetic of their websites, and effectively communicate their ideas. This section explores how bloggers utilize Midjourney to transform their posts through compelling visual storytelling, ultimately enriching their readers' experience.

One common application of Midjourney among bloggers is the creation of custom featured images. In a crowded digital landscape, a captivating featured image can significantly impact a blog's click-through rate. For instance, a travel blogger may use Midjourney to generate a stunning landscape that captures the essence of a destination they are writing about. Instead of relying solely on stock photos, which may lack uniqueness, they can create an original visual that embodies their personal style and perspective, making their content more appealing and engaging to potential readers.

Another innovative use of Midjourney is in crafting infographics or visual summaries of blog content. Bloggers who write about complex topics, such as technology or finance, can use AI-generated visuals to distill intricate information into easily digestible formats. For example, a tech blogger might create an infographic that illustrates the features of a new gadget using Midjourney, allowing readers to grasp key points at a glance. This not only enhances the informational value of the post but also encourages sharing on social media, as visually appealing content tends to attract more attention.

Midjourney allows bloggers to experiment with illustrative elements that complement their writing. A food blogger, for instance, could generate vibrant images of dishes that aren't available in their local area or create whimsical illustrations of ingredients. These visuals can add a layer of creativity, making posts feel more personal and inviting. By integrating these unique images, content creators can foster a stronger connection with their readers, inviting them into their world and encouraging them to explore the content further.

Bloggers can utilize Midjourney to maintain a consistent visual theme across their platforms. Branding is crucial in the blogging world, and having a cohesive aesthetic helps establish identity and recognition. By generating a series of images with similar styles, colors, and themes using Midjourney, bloggers can create a distinctive visual language that aligns with their content. This not only reinforces their brand but also provides a more enjoyable browsing experience for readers, who come to associate specific visuals with the blogger's unique voice and perspective.

In summary, Midjourney offers bloggers a versatile and innovative means to enhance their content through AI-generated visuals. From custom featured images to infographics and imaginative illustrations, the possibilities are vast. By creatively integrating these visuals, bloggers can elevate their storytelling, engage their audience more effectively, and establish a recognizable brand identity. As the digital landscape continues to evolve, embracing such tools will empower bloggers to stay ahead and captivate their readers in new and exciting ways.

Graphic Designers and AI

The integration of artificial intelligence (AI) in graphic design has transformed traditional workflows, enabling designers to explore new creative horizons. Midjourney, an innovative AI-driven image generation tool, stands at the forefront of this evolution. By harnessing the power of Midjourney, graphic designers can streamline their creative processes, enhance their productivity, and expand their artistic capabilities.

One of the most notable contributions of Midjourney to graphic design is its ability to generate unique logo concepts rapidly. Traditional logo design can be a time-consuming process, often involving extensive brainstorming and multiple iterations. Midjourney simplifies this by allowing designers to input specific parameters and keywords that reflect their brand's identity. The AI then produces a range of logo options, each with distinct styles and color palettes. This not only accelerates the design process but also inspires designers to think outside the box, leading to innovative branding solutions that might not have emerged through conventional methods.

Beyond logos, Midjourney plays a significant role in creating visually compelling advertisements. The ability to generate high-quality images tailored to specific marketing campaigns allows graphic designers to produce eye-catching visuals that resonate with target audiences. By utilizing Midjourney's capabilities, designers can experiment with various themes, layouts, and imagery, enabling them to craft advertisements that stand out in a crowded marketplace. This versatility not only saves time but also enhances the overall impact of marketing efforts, as designers can quickly iterate on ideas and refine their concepts based on real-time feedback.

Midjourney facilitates collaboration among designers and clients. In the past, conveying visual ideas to clients often involved lengthy explanations and back-and-forth communication. With AI-generated images, designers can present their concepts more vividly, providing clients with a clearer understanding of the proposed designs. This visual communication fosters more productive discussions, allowing for quicker approvals and adjustments. As a result, design projects can progress more smoothly, ultimately benefiting both designers and their clients.

The integration of Midjourney into graphic design also raises important considerations regarding originality and copyright. While AI generates images based on existing styles and techniques, designers must remain mindful of the ethical implications of using AI-generated content. Understanding how to effectively incorporate Midjourney's output into their work while maintaining a unique artistic vision is crucial for graphic designers. By blending their skills with AI capabilities, designers can push the boundaries of creativity while ensuring their work remains authentic and original.

Midjourney represents a significant advancement in the field of graphic design, offering a powerful tool for logo creation, advertisement design, and collaborative processes. As designers embrace this technology, they can enhance their creativity and efficiency while navigating the challenges that come with AI-driven art. By understanding how to utilize Midjourney effectively, graphic designers can not only improve their workflow but also redefine the possibilities of visual communication in the digital age.

Artists and Creative Projects

Artists, whether professionals or hobbyists, have increasingly turned to Midjourney as a versatile tool for generating images that can elevate their creative projects. This innovative platform allows users to harness the power of artificial intelligence to create visually compelling artwork, making it an attractive option for a diverse range of artistic endeavors. From concept development to final execution, Midjourney serves as a catalyst that enhances the creative process, enabling artists to explore new ideas and visual styles that they may not have considered otherwise.

For professional artists, Midjourney offers a unique opportunity to expand their portfolios and reach new audiences. Many professionals utilize the platform to generate preliminary sketches or concept art for larger projects, such as exhibitions or commissioned works. By experimenting with different prompts and styles, artists can quickly visualize their ideas, making the process of refining their concepts more efficient. This not only saves time but also allows for greater experimentation, as artists can explore a wide array of artistic directions without the constraints of traditional media.

Hobbyist artists, on the other hand, often find in Midjourney a means of expressing their creativity without the pressure of commercial success. The accessibility of the platform democratizes art-making, allowing individuals to create stunning visuals simply for the joy of creation.

Many hobbyists use Midjourney to explore personal themes or interests, generating images that resonate with their unique perspectives. This freedom can lead to unexpected artistic breakthroughs, as users discover new techniques and styles that enhance their overall creative practice.

Exhibitions and showcases represent another significant area where Midjourney's capabilities can be leveraged. Artists can create cohesive bodies of work that reflect a particular theme or narrative, using the platform to generate a series of related images. This can be particularly beneficial for group exhibitions, where a consistent visual language can strengthen the overall impact of the presentation. Additionally, digital exhibitions and online platforms have become increasingly popular, enabling artists to share their Midjourney-generated works with a global audience, thus expanding their reach and influence.

Finally, commissions provide an exciting avenue for artists to integrate Midjourney into their workflows. Many clients appreciate the artistic versatility that AI-generated images can offer, allowing for a collaborative approach where artists can iterate on ideas with unprecedented speed. Artists can present clients with multiple visual options based on their specifications, streamlining the decision-making process. This not only enhances client satisfaction but also enables artists to maintain their creative integrity while meeting commercial needs. As Midjourney continues to evolve, its role in the art community is likely to grow, offering even more innovative possibilities for both professional and hobbyist artists alike.

Chapter 9: Troubleshooting Common Issues

Common Problems and Solutions

In the evolving landscape of digital image generation using tools like Midjourney, users often encounter a variety of common problems that can hinder their creative process. Understanding these challenges is essential for anyone looking to harness the full potential of Midjourney, whether you're a blogger, content creator, artist, or graphic designer.

One prevalent issue faced by users is the generation of low-quality images. This can stem from several factors, including insufficient prompt detail or the inherent limitations of the tool. To resolve this, start by refining your input prompts. Aim for specificity by including adjectives that describe the style, colors, and elements you wish to see in your image. For example, instead of simply stating "a landscape," try "a vibrant sunset over a tranquil lake surrounded by mountains." Additionally, consider experimenting with the resolution settings, ensuring you select a higher resolution option if available. This not only enhances the clarity of your images but also provides more detail and depth.

Errors during the image generation process can also be a significant hurdle. These errors may occur due to server issues, incorrect prompt formats, or even glitches within the platform. To troubleshoot this, first check the official Midjourney support channels for any ongoing outages or maintenance updates. If everything appears operational, double-check your prompts for any syntax errors or unsupported characters. A good practice is to simplify your prompts if you encounter recurring errors, gradually adding complexity as you identify what works. Restarting the application or refreshing your session can also resolve temporary glitches that may hinder your image creation.

Another challenge that users frequently report is difficulty in achieving the desired style or output. This can be frustrating, especially when the generated images do not align with your vision. To address this, it's beneficial to study and analyze the types of prompts that yield successful results. Engage with the Midjourney community, where users often share their prompts and outcomes, offering insights into effective phrasing. When crafting your prompt, consider including reference images or style influences that align with your vision. This not only provides context for the algorithm but also increases the likelihood of generating an image that resonates with your intent.

Users may experience issues with image variations and consistency. When generating a series of images, you may find that they lack cohesiveness or diverge from your initial concept. To maintain consistency, utilize seed numbers in your prompts to replicate the same starting conditions for each generation. When refining your images, use the variation feature strategically. By selecting a base image you like and generating variations from it, you can explore different interpretations while still staying within a cohesive theme. This method fosters a more controlled and iterative approach to your creative output.

By understanding these common problems and implementing the solutions outlined here, users can navigate the complexities of Midjourney image generation with confidence. Whether you're creating stunning visuals for a blog, enhancing your artistic portfolio, or designing graphics for your next project, these strategies will equip you to tackle challenges head-on. Embrace the learning process, engage with the community, and continue to refine your techniques as you transform your concepts into captivating creations.

Maximizing Image Quality

Maximizing image quality in Midjourney is essential for anyone looking to create visually stunning content. The quality of generated images can significantly impact the viewer's perception and engagement, making it crucial to understand the nuances of prompt refinement and parameter adjustments.

One of the most effective ways to improve image quality is through prompt refinement. A well-structured prompt can lead to more accurate and visually appealing results. Start by being specific about the desired elements in the image. Instead of using vague terms, incorporate descriptive language that conveys the style, mood, and attributes you envision. For instance, instead of asking for a "landscape," specify "a serene mountain landscape at sunrise with a clear blue sky and lush greenery." This level of detail helps the Midjourney model understand your intent, leading to higher quality outputs.

In addition to refining prompts, adjusting the parameters provided by Midjourney can also make a significant difference in image quality. Familiarize yourself with the various parameters available, such as aspect ratio and quality settings. The aspect ratio can dramatically alter the composition of the image, so choose one that aligns with your vision. Similarly, adjusting the quality parameter can enhance the resolution and detail of the output, allowing for richer textures and more vibrant colors. Experimenting with these settings can lead to remarkable improvements, particularly when producing images for professional use.

Another crucial aspect of maximizing image quality is iterative generation. After receiving an initial image, take the time to assess what aspects meet your expectations and what could be improved. Use this feedback to modify your prompts or parameters for subsequent generations. This iterative process is fundamental to honing your skills in Midjourney and can lead to progressively better results. Don't hesitate to explore variations, as sometimes a subtle change can yield a vastly different and more satisfying outcome.

Consider the use of reference images to guide the generation process. Providing Midjourney with reference images can enhance its understanding of your desired style and subject matter. When uploading a reference image, ensure it aligns closely with the vision you have for your project. This practice can serve to anchor the generated output in a specific aesthetic, making it easier to achieve the quality you seek. Combining reference images with well-crafted prompts allows for a more directed and controlled image generation experience.

Maximizing image quality in Midjourney involves a multifaceted approach that includes refining prompts, adjusting parameters, engaging in iterative generation, and utilizing reference images. By implementing these strategies, users can significantly enhance the visual appeal of their generated images. Whether you are a blogger, content creator, artist, or graphic designer, these tips will empower you to create stunning visuals that resonate with your audience and elevate your creative projects.

Frequently Asked Questions

In the rapidly evolving world of image generation, especially with tools like Midjourney, newcomers often find themselves inundated with questions. This section aims to address the most common inquiries from beginners, providing clear and concise answers to help you navigate the initial steps of using Midjourney effectively. Understanding these foundational concepts will not only boost your confidence but also enhance your creative journey.

One of the most frequently asked questions is, "What is Midjourney, and how does it work?" Midjourney is an AI-powered platform designed to generate images based on textual prompts. Users input descriptions of what they envision, and the AI interprets these prompts to create unique visual representations. This process involves complex algorithms that analyze language and imagery, enabling the software to produce artistic outputs. Getting started is as simple as signing up for an account and familiarizing yourself with the interface.

Another common question is, "What types of images can I create with Midjourney?" The possibilities are virtually limitless. From abstract art and landscapes to character designs and product mockups, Midjourney caters to various creative needs. To maximize your results, focus on crafting detailed prompts that include specific elements you want to see in the image. The more descriptive you are, the better the AI can understand and generate your desired outcome. Experimenting with different styles and themes can also yield fascinating results.

Beginners often wonder, "How can I improve the quality of the images I generate?" To enhance your results, consider experimenting with different prompt structures and keywords. Understanding how to manipulate the input can significantly affect the output. Additionally, observing the images produced by others in the Midjourney community can provide inspiration and insight into effective techniques. Engaging with the community through forums or social media groups can also be an invaluable resource for learning and improving your skills.

Many newcomers ask, "Are there any costs associated with using Midjourney?" While Midjourney offers a free trial, continued use generally requires a subscription. This subscription grants access to premium features and higher-quality image generation. It is essential to weigh the options based on your needs and how frequently you plan to use the platform. Keep in mind that investing in a subscription can open up more advanced capabilities and tools that can significantly enhance your image generation experience.

By addressing these frequently asked questions, this section aims to demystify the initial stages of using Midjourney. As you continue to explore and experiment with this powerful tool, remember that creativity often thrives on curiosity and practice. Embrace the learning process, and don't hesitate to seek out additional resources and community support to further refine your image generation skills.

Chapter 10: The Future of Image Generation

AI and the Future of Content Creation

The advent of artificial intelligence has catalyzed transformative changes across various industries, particularly in content creation. Among the most prominent developments is the emergence of AI-generated imagery, which is reshaping how marketers, entertainers, and artists approach their crafts. The capabilities of tools like Midjourney have made it possible for users to generate high-quality images in a fraction of the time it would take using traditional methods. This shift not only enhances creativity but also democratizes access to advanced design techniques, allowing individuals with varying levels of expertise to produce compelling visuals.

In the marketing industry, AI-generated imagery is revolutionizing how brands engage with their audiences. By leveraging tools like Midjourney, marketers can create tailored visuals that resonate with specific demographics, resulting in more effective campaigns. The ability to generate diverse image styles and concepts quickly enables brands to test multiple creative approaches, optimizing their messaging based on real-time feedback. This agility not only improves the efficiency of marketing efforts but also enhances the overall consumer experience, as audiences are presented with content that feels more relevant and personalized.

The entertainment sector is also experiencing a dramatic shift due to the rise of AI-generated imagery. Filmmakers, game developers, and artists are incorporating these technologies to streamline their creative processes. For instance, concept artists can use Midjourney to rapidly visualize scenes or characters, providing a rich foundation upon which further artistic development can occur. This not only expedites production timelines but also opens up new avenues for storytelling, as creators can explore concepts that might have been impractical or too costly to produce traditionally. Consequently, the boundaries of creativity are being pushed as artists harness AI to realize their visions more fully.

The integration of AI in content creation raises important questions about originality and ownership. As tools like Midjourney produce stunning imagery based on user inputs, the line between human creativity and machine-generated content becomes increasingly blurred. This shift necessitates a reevaluation of copyright laws and ethical considerations surrounding the use of AI-generated images in various contexts. Content creators, bloggers, and graphic designers must navigate these evolving landscapes carefully, ensuring that they adhere to legal standards while also embracing the innovative potential of AI technologies.

As we look to the future, it is clear that AI-generated imagery will play a pivotal role in shaping the landscape of content creation. For those interested in using tools like Midjourney, staying abreast of emerging trends and best practices will be crucial. By understanding how these advancements can be effectively integrated into their workflows, content creators can harness the power of AI to elevate their artistry and engage their audiences in unprecedented ways. The journey from concept to creation is being redefined, and those willing to adapt will find themselves at the forefront of this exciting evolution in the creative industry.

The Evolution of Midjourney

The evolution of Midjourney has been marked by a series of advancements that have significantly enhanced its capabilities in image generation. Initially, the platform focused on creating stunning visuals from textual prompts, tapping into the potential of artificial intelligence to interpret user inputs creatively. As the technology has matured, Midjourney has integrated more sophisticated algorithms and machine learning techniques, allowing for improved accuracy and a wider range of artistic styles. This evolution is not merely a testament to technological progress but also a reflection of the growing needs and expectations of its user base, which includes bloggers, content creators, artists, and graphic designers.

Looking ahead, one of the most notable predictions for Midjourney's development is the incorporation of real-time collaboration features. As more users begin to adopt the platform for various projects, the ability to work together in real-time could enhance creative processes and streamline workflows. For instance, artists and graphic designers could collaborate seamlessly on a single image, sharing ideas and making adjustments instantaneously. This collaborative approach could foster a community-driven environment, encouraging users to exchange techniques and tips, ultimately enriching the creative output facilitated by Midjourney.

Another area ripe for evolution is the personalization of image generation. As artificial intelligence becomes increasingly adept at understanding individual user preferences, Midjourney could implement features that allow for personalized style filters and customized templates. This would enable users to generate images that not only meet their creative needs but also reflect their unique artistic voice. For content creators and bloggers, such customization could significantly enhance brand identity, allowing for a distinct visual language that resonates with their audience.

Advancements in AI-driven content understanding could lead to the integration of multimedia elements within Midjourney. The platform may evolve to allow users to generate not only static images but also dynamic content such as animations or interactive visuals. By incorporating motion and interactivity, Midjourney could open new avenues for storytelling and engagement, particularly beneficial for digital marketers and educators seeking to captivate their audiences. This shift would mark a significant step in the evolution of image generation, transforming static visuals into immersive experiences.

As ethical considerations surrounding AI-generated content continue to evolve, Midjourney will likely need to incorporate features that promote responsible usage. This may include tools for watermarking images, copyright management, and guidelines for ethical image generation. By adopting such measures, Midjourney can help ensure that its users engage with the technology in a way that respects artistic integrity and intellectual property rights. As the platform evolves, fostering a culture of ethical creativity will be paramount, enabling users to harness the power of AI responsibly and innovatively.

Opportunities for Content Creators

The landscape of content creation is rapidly evolving, and artificial intelligence (AI) is at the forefront of this transformation. For creators, particularly those utilizing tools like Midjourney, the future promises a wealth of opportunities that can enhance their work. As AI continues to develop, it opens new avenues for creativity, efficiency, and personalization. Understanding how to leverage these advancements can significantly impact the quality and reach of a creator's output.

One of the most promising aspects of future AI developments is the ability to create more sophisticated image generation models. Midjourney, as a platform, is already leading the way in providing high-quality visual content. However, as AI algorithms advance, creators can expect even more nuanced control over the images they generate. This means that artists and designers can manipulate elements such as style, composition, and color palettes with unprecedented precision, allowing for a more tailored artistic expression. Embracing these technologies will empower content creators to push the boundaries of their imagination.

AI advancements are likely to enhance the collaborative process between creators and the technology they use. Future iterations of Midjourney may incorporate features that allow for real-time feedback and adaptation, enabling creators to experiment with multiple iterations of their ideas quickly. This interactive capability can streamline the creative workflow, making it easier to refine concepts and produce polished final products. By harnessing these tools, creators can focus more on ideation and less on technical execution, ultimately resulting in a richer creative process.

Personalization is another area where AI is poised to make a significant impact. As algorithms become more adept at analyzing user preferences and behavior, content creators will be able to generate images that resonate more deeply with their target audiences. This capability can lead to improved engagement and connection with viewers, as creators can produce visuals that align closely with the interests and emotions of their followers. For bloggers and social media influencers, this means crafting content that not only stands out visually but also speaks directly to the needs and desires of their audience.

In addition to enhancing image generation and personalization, future AI developments are likely to facilitate better integration with other digital tools and platforms. As the ecosystem of content creation tools expands, seamless interoperability will become increasingly important. Creators using Midjourney will benefit from enhanced compatibility with various content management systems, social media platforms, and marketing tools. This synergy will allow for smoother workflows and more effective distribution of visual content, ultimately amplifying a creator's reach and impact in the digital landscape.

In summary, the future of AI presents a multitude of opportunities for content creators using Midjourney for image generation. By staying informed about these developments and actively seeking ways to integrate them into their work, creators can enhance their artistic capabilities, streamline their processes, and foster deeper connections with their audiences. The journey from concept to creation is evolving, and those who embrace these changes will be well-positioned to thrive in an increasingly dynamic digital environment.

Chapter 11: Conclusion and Next Steps

Key Takeaways

In "From Concept to Creation: A Practical Guide to Midjourney Image Generation," several essential principles and techniques are highlighted to empower users in their image generation endeavors. The book serves as a comprehensive resource for individuals interested in leveraging Midjourney for creative outputs, whether they are bloggers, content creators, artists, or graphic designers. A foundational understanding of the capabilities and functionalities of Midjourney is crucial, as it enables users to harness the platform's potential effectively. By familiarizing themselves with the interface and the types of prompts that yield the best results, readers will be better equipped to produce stunning visuals tailored to their specific needs.

One of the key takeaways from this guide is the importance of crafting precise and descriptive prompts. The way users articulate their ideas directly influences the quality and relevance of the generated images. The book emphasizes the balance between specificity and creativity, encouraging users to experiment with various prompt styles. By incorporating detailed descriptions and desired artistic styles, users can guide the image generation process to align more closely with their vision. This understanding of prompt engineering is vital for anyone looking to create unique and impactful images.

The book delves into the significance of iterative experimentation. Midjourney's image generation capabilities thrive on a trial-and-error approach, where users are encouraged to refine their prompts based on the outcomes they receive. This iterative process not only enhances the quality of the images but also cultivates a deeper understanding of how different variables affect the final output. Readers are encouraged to embrace mistakes as learning opportunities, fostering a growth mindset that is essential for mastering any creative tool.

Another important point covered is the diverse range of applications for Midjourney across various fields. Whether for blog illustrations, social media content, or artistic projects, the flexibility of Midjourney allows users to adapt their image generation techniques to fit their unique objectives. The book highlights case studies and examples showcasing how different professionals have successfully integrated Midjourney into their workflows, providing inspiration and practical insights for readers to apply in their own projects.

Finally, the book underscores the ethical considerations surrounding image generation technology. As users explore the vast possibilities of Midjourney, it is crucial to remain mindful of copyright, originality, and the responsible use of AI-generated content. The guide encourages readers to develop a strong ethical framework for their creative practices, ensuring that their work respects both artistic integrity and the rights of others. By integrating these key takeaways into their creative processes, users will be well-positioned to transform their concepts into compelling visual narratives using Midjourney.

Resources for Continued Learning

As you embark on your journey of image generation using Midjourney, it is essential to recognize that the learning process does not end with the basics. The field of digital art and AI-driven image creation is constantly evolving, offering new techniques, tools, and insights.

Engaging with these resources will allow you to deepen your understanding, experiment with new ideas, and connect with fellow creators.

One of the best places to start is the official Midjourney documentation and tutorial section. This resource offers a comprehensive overview of the platform's features, functionalities, and best practices. Engaging with these tutorials can help you grasp the core principles of image generation, from understanding prompts to utilizing advanced settings. You can find these resources directly on the Midjourney website, where they provide step-by-step guides and visual examples. YouTube hosts a myriad of video tutorials created by experienced users, providing visual learners with practical insights into the processes of image generation and creative experimentation.

To foster a sense of community and collaboration, consider joining online forums and discussion groups focused on Midjourney. Platforms such as Reddit and Discord have dedicated channels where users share their works, discuss techniques, and provide feedback on each other's creations. Participating in these communities can inspire you to explore new ideas and approaches, as well as give you the opportunity to ask questions and seek advice from more experienced artists and designers. These interactions can significantly enhance your learning experience and help you stay motivated on your creative journey.

Furthermore, many blogs and websites are dedicated to digital art and AI technologies, offering articles, tips, and insights relevant to Midjourney users. Websites like Medium and ArtStation often feature contributions from artists who share their experiences and techniques. Subscribing to these platforms can keep you updated on the latest trends and innovations in image generation. Additionally, attending webinars and online workshops hosted by industry professionals can provide you with hands-on experience and networking opportunities that can prove invaluable for your growth as a content creator.

Consider exploring social media platforms such as Instagram and Twitter, where artists frequently showcase their work and share insights into their creative processes. Following hashtags like #MidjourneyArt or #AIArt can connect you with a wider community of creators and expose you to diverse techniques and styles. Engaging in these platforms allows for a continuous flow of inspiration and knowledge, encouraging you to experiment with the tips and techniques you learn. By leveraging these resources, you can ensure that your journey with Midjourney remains dynamic and enriching, ultimately leading to the creation of stunning, innovative images.

Start Creating!

Creating images with Midjourney opens an exciting door to endless possibilities for expression and engagement. As you explore this innovative platform, you will find that it is designed to cater to a wide range of users, from bloggers and content creators to artists and graphic designers. Each individual brings a unique perspective and set of skills that can be enhanced by utilizing Midjourney's advanced image generation capabilities. This is your opportunity to not only enhance your creative output but also establish a distinctive visual identity in your work.

The process of generating images with Midjourney is accessible and intuitive, making it an excellent tool for both beginners and seasoned creators. Understanding the basic image generation techniques is crucial, as it serves as the foundation for more complex projects. By familiarizing yourself with the platform's features, such as prompt crafting, style selection, and parameter adjustments, you can unlock a powerful creative tool that will elevate your visual content. The journey from concept to creation is a fulfilling one, where each image you generate can serve as a stepping stone toward mastering your craft.

As you delve into the intricacies of Midjourney, remember that experimentation is key. The beauty of this platform lies in its ability to respond to your creative instincts. Don't hesitate to play with different prompts and styles, observing how subtle changes can yield dramatically different results. This trial-and-error approach will not only enhance your understanding of the tool but also inspire new ideas and concepts that you may not have initially considered. Each experiment is a learning opportunity that pushes you closer to your unique artistic vision.

Community plays an essential role in the creative process, and Midjourney boasts a vibrant user base that is eager to share insights and experiences. Engaging with fellow creatives can provide valuable feedback and inspiration, allowing you to refine your techniques and expand your horizons. Whether you choose to participate in forums, social media groups, or collaborative projects, connecting with others can enrich your journey and foster a sense of belonging within the creative landscape.

As you stand on the brink of your creative journey with Midjourney, remember that every great creator started somewhere. The key is to take that first step. Embrace the learning curve, welcome the challenges, and celebrate the victories, no matter how small. Your unique perspective and creativity deserve to be expressed, and Midjourney is the perfect medium to bring your ideas to life. Dive in, experiment fearlessly, and allow your imagination to flourish—your next masterpiece awaits!

www.ingramcontent.com/pod-product-compliance
Lightning Source LLC
LaVergne TN
LVHW051608050326
832903LV00033B/4402